A Bunch of
POESY

A Bunch of POESY

Leunig

Angus&Robertson
An imprint of HarperCollins*Publishers*

TO

ACKNOWLEDGMENTS

These poems emerged over twenty-two years from
my work on the *Age* and *Nation Review* newspapers.
My thanks to their editors.

M L

CONTENTS

SEASONS & CELEBRATIONS 57

Life &
CIRCUMSTANCE

Life

When life goes by so quickly
That you feel you're just a blur
Then mumble vaguely to yourself
Sort of, 'umm . . . umm . . . errr . . .'

There's a Bird at the Window

There's a bird at the window

A wolf at the door

A fly in the ointment

A snake on the floor

A flower on the pillow

A note on the bed

In the spare room attached

To the back of my head

A Boomerang

Between the whimper and the bang
Life is like a boomerang
Thrown by some great hairy hand
Spinning out across the land
Spinning out across the years
Spinning lies and spinning tears
Spinning heart and spinning brain
Spinning pleasure, spinning pain
Spinning out and spinning round
And spinning back towards the ground
A graceful loop across the land
Then back into the hairy hand

How to Hold on to It

Hold on to it like
you hold a day old
chicken

Hold on to it like
you hold a live fish.

Hold on to it like you
hold a horse.

Hold on to it like you
hold a bowl of soup.

Hold on to it like you
hold a door open for
the Queen Mother.

Letting go of it is
just as difficult and
shall be dealt with
at some later stage.

How to Get There

Go to the end of the
path until you get to
the gate.

Go through the gate
and head straight out
towards the horizon.

Keep going towards
the horizon.

Sit down and have
a rest every now
and again.

But keep on going.
Just keep on with it

keep on going as
far as you can.
That's how you
get there

The Tiny Boat

God bless this tiny little boat
And me who travels in it
It stays afloat for years and years
And sinks within a minute.

And so the soul in which we sail
Unknown by years of thinking,
Is deeply felt and understood
The minute that it's sinking.

The Dream

Down I lay in a boat on the bay
And I dreamed about friends of the past
And while I was sleeping
The dream upward creeping
Had fastened itself to the mast

So blow all ye gales and fill up my sails
And carry me far, far away
Til my billowing dreams
All burst at the seams
As I lie in a boat on the bay

A Winter's Saturday Afternoon in Melbourne

In an old masonic hall

I saw a bum upon a wall

I saw its mournful, aimless stare

And saw that life was cold and bare

Life 2

Life's a jigsaw puzzle . . .

Some do it in reverse

They take a pretty picture

And make it all diverse

A Child is a Grub

A child is a grub

And a man's a cocoon

Music's a butterfly . . .

Sing me a tune

When the Heart is Cut

When the heart
Is cut or cracked or broken
Do not clutch it
Let the wound lie open

Let the wind
From the good old sea blow in
To bathe the wound with salt
And let it sting

Let a stray dog lick it
Let a bird lean in the hole and sing
A simple song like a tiny bell
And let it ring

Personal, Social and Domestic Vulcanology

The head.

The heart.

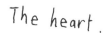

The hands.

The home.

Possible Forthcoming Eruptions

The car.

The television.

The people.

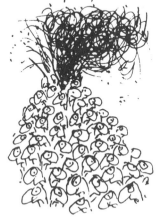

.... but not the dog.
Never the dog.

The Old Lover

Why do you weep you poor, sad, old tree
I've lost an old lover, I'm weeping for me
But what are you saying, you know we love you
Yes I'm popular now but this love was true
This was a love from a difficult time
When the love of a tree had no reason or rhyme
No profit or motive of saving the earth
A love 'unimportant, of dubious worth'
A nuisance, escapist, naïve or insane
Loopy and lonely and hard to explain
So my lover went off with a faraway stare
And is lost among all this new passion and care
And although I'm respected I'll always be sad
At the loss of a love just a tiny bit mad

Things Just Seem to Fall Apart

Things just seem to fall apart
String bags full of oranges
And things within the heart
Calamities evaporate and memories depart
People laugh at anything
And things just fall apart

The Mirror

Each year my mirror seems much older
Somewhat duller and a fraction colder
The glass which always gleamed and twinkled
Now appears all scratched and wrinkled

Appears more blotchy, tired and droopy
Confused and haggard, tired and loopy
Sadder, slower, grimmer, glummer
I think that I've been sold a bummer

Sitting on the Fence

Come sit down beside me

I said to myself

And although it doesn't make sense,

I held my own hand

As a small sign of trust

And together I sat on the fence

The Facts of Life

WHERE DO BABIES GO TO....?

WILL SOMEBODY EXPLAIN

THEY GO INTO THE WORLD . . . .

AND THEN . . . THEY'RE NEVER SEEN AGAIN.

The Path to Your Door

The path to your door

Is the path within;

Is made by animals,

Is lined by flowers,

Is lined by thorns,

Is stained by wine,

Is lit by the lamp of sorrowful dreams:

Is washed with joy,

Is swept by grief,

Is blessed by the lonely traffic of art:

Is known by heart,

Is known by prayer,

Is lost and found,

Is always strange,

The path to your door.

The Search

We search and we search and yet find no meaning.

The search for a meaning leads to despair.

And when we are broken the heart finds its moment

To fly and to feel and to work as it will

Through the darkness and mystery and wild contradiction.

For this is its freedom, its need and its calling;

This is its magic, its strength and its knowing.

To heal and make meaning while we walk or lie dreaming;

To give birth to love within our surrender;

To mother our faith, our spirit and yearning;

While we stumble in darkness the heart makes our meaning

And offers it into our life and creation

That we may give meaning to life and creation

For we only give meaning we do not find meaning:

The thing we can't find is the thing we shall give.

To make love complete and to honour creation.

Let it Go

Let it go. Let it out.

Let it all unravel.

Let it free and it can be

A path on which to travel.

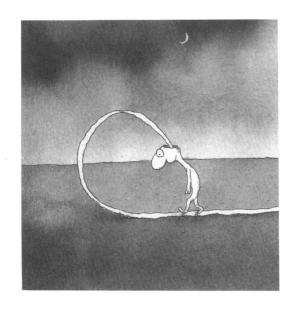

A Tiny Piece of Gravel

Oh ... my goodness..
it's so beautiful..

just a tiny piece
of gravel in the brick..
but it's so perfect..

It catches the light...
It glistens....
It gleams.

I see heavenly
colors...
my head
swims...
my vision
blurrs...

I see the universe...
...everything makes sense...

It's magical...
... wonderful...
it's beautiful...

A Dusty Little Swag

All my father left me

Was a dusty little swag

And a pair of tiny booties

In a crumpled paper bag

And he left me in confusion

And he left me in despair

And he left the swag and booties

For the walk to god knows where.

Doom &
GLOOM

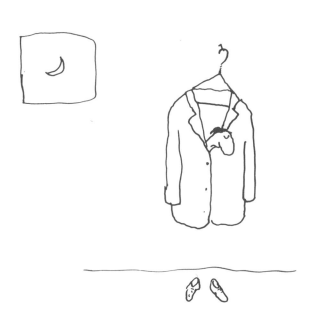

Now I Lay Me Down to Sleep

Now I lay me down to sleep
I pray thee lord my soul to sweep
Yes sweep it with your mighty broom
Until it's like a tidy room
All neat and clean with doors shut tight
And curtains drawn against the light
The neatest, darkest piece of gloom
My soul, my locked and empty room

The Wagon of Hope

The wagon of hope
Is pulled by ducks
Two fine ducks
As white as snow

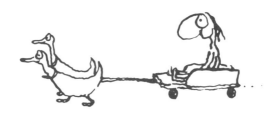

The boat of faith
Is kept afloat
By stars above
And fish below

The way ahead
Is known to birds
Is told by birds
Each day at dawn

While the song of doom
Composed by men
Is played upon
A paper horn

Read All About It

Read all about it in twenty years time
When those who survive become sad:
When the lime has consumed
What the maggots passed up
And the New Order starts to go mad

Yes, read all about it at some later stage
When those who remain have grown old:
When they hear a strange bell
From a lone inner hell
And the New Order starts to go cold.

We'll read all about it, the deathbed confession,

And see it as no contradiction

For it seems the New Order

Recognises no border

Between what is fact and is fiction

So we'll read all about it and read all about it

As we've read all about it before.

When the facts come to light

It's the same endless plight

The disorder of New Order war.

The People's Treasure

They're privatising things we own together.
They're flogging off the people's common ground.
And though we're still connected by the weather
They say that sharing things is now unsound

They're lonelifying all the public spaces
They're rationalising swags and billabongs
They're awfulising nature's lovely places
Dismantling the dreaming and the songs

Their macho fear of flabby, soft sensations
Makes them pine for all things hard and lean
They talk of foreign market penetrations
And throbbing private sectors. It's obscene.

They're basically unloving types of creatures
With demons lurking underneath their beds
You'll notice that a necktie always features
To keep their hearts quite separate from their heads

So if they steal away the people's treasure
And bring the jolly swagman to his knees
They can't remove the simple, common pleasure
Of loathing public bastards such as these

Awfulise
Awfulisation
To be an Awfuliser

Every night and every day

The awfulisers work away

Awfulising public places,

Favourite things and little graces

Awfulising lovely treasures

Common joys and simple pleasures

Awfulising far and near

The parts of life we held so dear

Democratic, clean and lawful

Awful, awful, awful, awful

Leadership Qualities

Our civic leaders are absolutely gaga
Our tribal elders are going 'round the twist
Our elder statesmen have all gone slightly ratty
And our wise old gurus simply can't exist

They've all gone wacko, cuckoo and bananas:
Troppo, loopy, screwy and up the wall:
Out the window, barmy and totally bonkers;
Cranky, batty, dotty; and that's not all!

They're carrying on like cut snakes and two-bob watches!
They're racing 'round like headless chooks and off their tree
They've blown a fuse, they're round the bend and off the planet.
And that's the most sophisticated political analysis you'll get from me.

The Missile

There is a missile, so I've heard
Which locks on to the smallest bird.
Finely tuned to seek and kill
A tiny chirp or gentle trill

It's modern warfare's answer to
An ancient wisdom tried and true:
When fighting wars you first destroy
All songs of innocence and joy

The Goode Knight

There was a good knight

Who rode a good horse

And he fought the good fight

In a good way, of course!

He was decent and rational

And sporting and nice.

No hint of bad habits.

No whisper of vice.

And his armour was sensible.

Clean and complete.

Not an improper gap

From his head to his feet.

Scientifically made

For the war against sin,

But what keeps the bad out

Also keeps the bad in

And bad that's kept in

Can make misery grow

And sometimes it's better

To let it all show

Not that I'm saying

The knight was so bad

But the tone of his voice

Grew suspiciously sad

As his troubles were growing

His victories were few

And they called it 'bad luck'

When his lance went askew

But the man who dares put

On the armour of good

And battles to make

The world be as it should

Can get out of balance

And waver off course

And mysteriously fall

Off the back of his horse.

The Wall

The great dividing wall came down
But it hasn't gone away;
It lies flat on the surface now
To keep what's underneath at bay;
And what's below our surface
Has become the 'other side'
More dreadful than the communists
Across the old divide
Yes the wall's been repositioned
And it's thick and strong and flat;
To keep us from the awful things
Swept underneath the mat

What AIDS Will Do to Your Sex Life

AIDS MEANS THE END OF
CASUAL SEX . SAY GOODBYE
TO THONGS AND T-SHIRT SEX ...

JOKING , FRIENDLY "HAVE A
CUP OF TEA " SEX . EXPERIMENTAL
JAZZY , CUBIST SEX

FREE FORM, OUTDOOR PEOPLE'S
STREET SEX. DROUGHTY, RURAL
MAKE-DO TIN SHED SEX.
  SAY GOODBYE TO ALL THAT.

SAY HELLO TO FORMAL SEX.

CLASSICAL, HIGHBROW, SERIOUS
MONOGAMOUS SEX.

DILIGENT, EXTERNALLY
EXAMINED AND ASSESSED
    THEORY AND PRAC.
WITH HONORS SEX

RESPONSIBLE, SENSIBLE
PHOTO-REALIST SEX. STRICTLY
STRUCTURED "BEGINNING,
MIDDLE AND END" SEX
ETC. ETC. ETC.
SAY HELLO TO ALL THAT.

The 1989 Melbourne Weeping Festival Programme

Sob and weep

By candlelight

Weep upwards

Into the night

Weep onto a sleeping mouse

Weep naked underneath the house

Weep among the dying trees

Weep down on your hands and knees

Weep with angels when you sleep

Softly gently

Weep weep weep

Repent

People crawl along streets

Lamp posts droop

Bus shelters wilt

Statues hang limply from pedestals

Spoons droop from cups

Teapot spouts flop on dirty old table cloths

Conductors' batons and violins sag

GLOOM AND DOOM . . .

everywhere things are declining.

Nest Eggs

Come all you battery chickens
With cramped up wings and legs
Prepare those aching bottoms
To lay some extra eggs

And do be warned my little fowls
The future could be bleak
They say retirement's awful
With an amputated beak

So make you preparations now
For when you leave the coop
We recommend the omelette
And not the chicken soup

And so my anxious feathered friends
My captive chickadees
Just brace those drumsticks one and all
And squeeze, squeeze, squeeze!

The Demon

WHEN I AWOKE THIS MORNING
EXHAUSTED FROM MY REST
A DEMON DARK AND TERRIBLE
WAS SITTING ON MY CHEST.

HE PINNED ME TO THE MATTRESS
AND SEIZED ME BY THE HEAD
HE PRESSED HIS KNEES AGAINST MY HEART
AND OVERTURNED THE BED.

HE DRAGGED ME TO THE MIRROR
AND SHOWED ME MY DISGRACE
THEN TOOK A RAZOR IN HIS CLAW
AND DRAGGED IT DOWN MY FACE

SOME FADED RAGS HE BOUND AROUND
MY SHOULDERS AND MY HIPS
AND POURED A CUP OF STEAMING MUCK
BETWEEN MY FADED LIPS

AND THEN HE TOOK THOSE WILTED LIPS
AND IN HIS EVIL STYLE
HE PARALYSED THE CORNERS UP
INTO A PLEASANT SMILE

A MASTERPIECE IN WICKEDNESS
THIS LAST SADISTIC JOKE
HE SENDS ME OUT INTO THE WORLD
A SMILING SORT OF BLOKE.

Musical Reform Package

Deregulate the orchestra
There's been too much protection.
A synthesiser does the job
Sack the woodwind section!

Restructure the 'Moonlight Sonata'
It's too soft! Go on, be bold!
Make it more competitive
It's far too slow and old.

Rationalise the violin
No one's going to starve.
Eliminate that curly bit
It takes too long to carve.

Seasons &
CELEBRATIONS

My Shoe

Since I hurt my pendulum

My life is all erratic

My parrot who was cordial

Is now transmitting static.

The carpet died, a palm collapsed,

The cat keeps doing poo

The only thing that keeps me sane

Is talking to my shoe.

Owed to Autumn

I had a pair of trousers
A jolly shade of green
I wore them in the summertime
And kept them bright and clean

Now autumn is upon us
My pants are turning gold
And soon they'll fall and blow away
To leave me bare and cold

Love

Love is born
With a dark and troubled face
When hope is dead
And in the most unlikely place
Love is born:
Love is always born.

A Christmas Carol

Frankincense is very fine

It elevates the soul

And myrrh will soothe a broken heart

And make the spirit whole

And though we like these gentle things

We're not entirely sold

The man who steals our heart away

Is the one who brings us heaps and heaps

And heaps and heaps of gold

Ode to Her Majesty

I did but see her passing by, she passed me by quite fast.

I saw her passing by again when several years had passed.

And then at some much later stage she passed me by once more

And there were further passings by and these I also saw.

I did but see her passing by I don't know what it means

Perhaps it's not my problem but a problem of the Queen's.

Ode to the Corgis

There's a marriage at the Palace
Which has lasted through the years
Between two little Royals there,
With furry, wing-like ears.
Unlike the ones who placed their trust
In reeking tube and iron shard
They trusted love and never found
That married life was all that hard.

So bring them to the Abbey now
In chariots of blazing fire.
Exalt their splendid doggy-style,
Their steaming arrows of desire.
The orb, the sceptre in their paws,
Beneath their tails a throne.
A crown of pearls upon their heads
And in their mouths a bone,
A crown of pearls with wing-like ears
And in their mouths a bone!

White

Peoples faces
turn white!

White knuckles.

White fangs.

The whites of
their eyes !

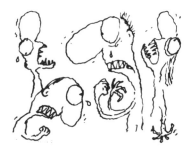

White pills.
White tablets

White rooms with
men in white coats.

White ambulances.
White bandages

WHITE CHRISTMAS !

The Absolute Grand Final

If I could change Australian rules,

If I could make a plan

I'd take three dozen footballs

And give one to each man

I'd place three dozen sets of posts

With a maximum of clearance

So each man kicks a feast of goals

Without an interference

And I'd make each game ten hours long

With a minimum of rest

And let them score until they're sore

And let the crowd all yell and roar

Until the whole thing seems a bore

And furthermore until they've got

The whole thing off their chest

A Tribute

With the barbie tongs he was a master

He could make a party stop

He could seize a blowfly in mid-flight

Then gently turn a chop

Roll a condom on a sausage

Causing male eyes to drop

All done with tongs made in Taiwan

He was an artist at the top

What Did We Get?

What did you get on your Christmas morn?
On the Christmas morn when you were born
Did you get some milk, did you get some pain,
Did you get some hurt that you can't explain?
Did you get a star from high above?
Did you get the gaze of a mother's love?
The spark that leaps from eye to eye
And twinkles 'til the day you die.

Oh what did we get on our Christmas morn
On the Christmas morn when we were born ...?

Christmas

Christmas is coming and the world is going barmy

Please prepare your son for the old man's army

If you haven't got a son then a daughter will do

If you haven't got a daughter then god bless you

Autumn

Autumn. It's autumn!
The sweet and sad post-mortem
The things we did last summer
That we'll never do again

Stranger and stranger
The cold and empty manger
The things we felt last summer
That we'll never feel again

A Winter's Poem

A clever creature is the snake
Who spends his winter not awake
He snuggles in his long thin bed
And brews up venom in his head

The human is a different sort
He spends the winter watching sport
He yells abuse in concrete stands
And empties out his poison glands

Owed to Spring

(B Y   A   G R U M P Y   M A N)

Gently now the sleeping trees awake
In innocence their wide green eyes do stare
At gypsy birds returning to their arms
And joyous bees just be without a care

I'm tired of spring, I've seen it all before
The same old song. In my cocoon I'll stew
While mother nature does her old routine
I'll desperate try to think of something new

Deepest Blue

(BRETT WHITELEY)

 Burke and Wills and Whiteley too
In visions of the deepest blue
Dreamed wildly of some inner sea
Where life they had not lived might be

And searching for this wondrous place
Made maps and paintings of a face
With graceful curves of dried up streams
By which the sea drained from their dreams

And so in lost and lonely camps
They spoke their prayers and snuffed their lamps
Burke and Wills and Whiteley too
Into the night of deepest blue.